THE DISG

Charles Boyle was born in Leeds in 1951. Between 1977 and 2001 he published six collections of poetry; he has also written fiction and non-fiction under the pen names Jennie Walker and Jack Robinson. In 2007 he founded the small press CB editions.

The Disguise

POEMS 1977–2001

Charles Boyle

selected by
CHRISTOPHER REID

CΛRCΛNET

First published in Great Britain in 2021 by
Carcanet
Alliance House, 30 Cross Street
Manchester M2 7AQ
www.carcanet.co.uk

A CIP catalogue record for this book is
available from the British Library.

ISBN 978 1 80017 028 5

Book design by Andrew Latimer
Printed in Great Britain by SRP Ltd, Exeter, Devon

The publisher acknowledges financial
assistance from Arts Council England.

CONTENTS

from *Affinities* (1977)

from *House of Cards* (1982)

from *Sleeping Rough* (1987)

from *The Very Man* (1993)

from *Paleface* (1996)

from *The Age of Cardboard and String* (2001)

THE DISGUISE

MOVING IN

The shape of the key is still strange in my hand.

Inside, all's silent and in shadow: a sense
of violating stillness as in a tomb.

We wander through, touching dust, pausing
to look, to listen, to watch each other's faces.

On the south side we find, as promised, the balcony.
you open the shutters, letting daylight in

on faded chairs, the worn carpet, a magazine.
There are pictures of flowers and eastern girls.

All this will have to go, you say. Less sure
than you, I fear displacing the old echoes.

FOREIGN CURFEW

Someone remembered the time. Someone tuned
to the World Service, we heard that outside
there were already thirty dead.

There seemed to be too many empty glasses.
When the news was off we returned
to word games, jokes, our music on cassette.

From the balcony the sky was unnaturally
clear; in the street below two cats
were stalking each other, maybe courting.

IN EGYPT

The sun in time-warped villages
turns a hallowed text, the same plot
each day, same talk of the elders
in their patch of shade, a fat bullock
lugs the waterwheel
in the old immutable circle.

A numb body, a blindness
to other galaxies, are the fruits
of worship. I cherish exposure, outcasts
and children, careless and trusting
on the eight-lane Cairo freeway
they dance with death.

ALEX IN FEBRUARY

The ex-king's palace is a museum now,
ragbag of swords and medals, French furniture,
an English pram; in the queen's bathroom
we gawp at antique plumbing.

We are as cold perhaps as she.
Out of season, this could be somewhere English,
a spitting rain in the off-sea wind,
sunlight glancing through the waves' fine spray.

A thin, brilliant mist hangs over the sea,
element at times of madness, a sleep of reason
whose monsters dog me, familiar and feigning tame,
they know the answers but they never tell.

No one it seems knows where the king has gone,
or if he's yet dead. Imagining, I sit
in a seafront café reading last week's English papers
as the clouds lumber across.

They split with hail: children sprint
across the blitzed Corniche, and the dark muffled Arabs
huddle at doors.
Exile's a disease, we catch it being born.

A PUBLIC DEATH

Flurry of wings, feathers, bones
in the dust, delirium of pain,
the amazed eyes –

I could disown it – and one life less
won't make the difference – the public death,
the generals, men of letters,
names from the books now classified obit:
the sparrow hit by a car
and tossed quite close to where I stand.
Sometimes the air is stirred and the wings
rise up, the wind still mocking flight,
as if what ended in the body's fall
was not a life, was nothing I could have known,
no subject mourned but vacancy of air.

As when I stared for minutes
at the bones of a pre-Christian child, bones
behind glass, the same intense
aesthetic fascination. As once,
stepping too quickly out of church, I slipped
on the wet stones – my father gripped my arm.

DOG DAYS AT COURT

The good king killed, his killer bedding queen,
revenge and madness in the true son's heart –

it is the custom of our time. All day
between the dawn's chill and the night's hot lust

we have waited, true servants, for our lord's
command, our cue for entrance to that scene

in which the false king dies and our own words
shall give to action such meaning as it has.

I have observed, told lies, committed incest
with the queen – her cries to me were music.

Outside our gate old peasants work the fields,
their lives as silent as unwritten books.

VISITING

Arriving with flowers it is like
a last anniversary, it is
like thanking the hostess one doesn't know.
They are something to hold.

Behind them, bleak pattern of branches
against a washed-out sky, my own parked car
beneath. When the lights turn red
you can sometimes hear the birds.

The blossom's early, I say –
you look up, the smile that cuts the edge,
not talking much because it tires the heart.
Daffodils, oranges, should not be here,

the room too cold, dust on the surface
of your standing water, old stains
on the wall above the radiator.
Once, seeing a stately four-poster,

I could die in a bed like this – here,
huddle of flesh beneath the bulk of sheets,
O my darling we seem,
we seem to have run out of choice.

A silent nurse rearranges my flowers.
The branches never move, imprinted on the sky.
I leave, guilty as usual
and still not knowing how not to feel it.

THE SCHOOL ATLAS

The geography teacher's smug monotone
is spliced with gunshots – a Messerschmitt 109
nose-dives into the North Sea, its pilot
still dangling beneath his parachute.

Other days were calmer, I'd doodle
sea monsters, a Mexican bandit with bandoliers,
or stare through the window at passing clouds
like continents unravelling…

I doubt the teacher himself, replaying
the same set syllabus year by year, ever hoped
for more. Boring us with statistics,
he made us look between the lines

into woodland or open fields where lovers
hide, a tramp falls asleep in the warmth
of a ditch, the surviving generations
lay out their baskets for a Sunday picnic.

Also those anonymous places we dreamed
our future in, named now and trapped in the web
with our precise addresses, as real
and inescapable as my random Osmiroid inkblots.

BED AND BREAKFAST

The weather affects you in certain ways
you won't or can't define: the raw, unshapely clouds
heading nowhere in particular are clouds
after all, indistinguishable from themselves.

The sea is locked away. 'Absentee landlord,' I attempt
to joke, but the situation is not funny at all,
the whole front is a sequence of lovers in cars
whose windscreen wipers say no, repeatedly.

We are sitting on the rocks with our bottle of supermarket wine
still arguing about the wallpaper, the bidet, whether the curtains
will open on the first act of a Verdi opera
or a clear blue sky, equally impossible.

The sun, as usual, has the last word,
dropping gently and slowly below the belt.
It teaches us nothing, but would be warmer I think
if we learned to be more tolerant of ourselves.

THE DRIFTING HOUSE

Early mornings, the mist
white shadow over all, hearing
a gull's cry and the secret lap, suck, thirst
of the unseen lake – till the house
came clean upon me, that high black house
built on the lakeshore by forgotten wealth,
still standing past its prime. I watched,
often uncertain in the widening scape
who's watching who, whose movement
scared the gulls; and then turned back
towards the road I'd left.

Attempting that shore, imagining again
my morning walks, the house recedes
as backdrop to the scene: the blue sky
and the silver lake, bright birds among the trees,
and women strolling in and out
through doors I never entered.

HOUSE OF CARDS

Ah there, there on the headland
is our fisherman's shack knocked together from planks and things
we have no other use for, there can be
no other use. Open to all weathers, vapours,
doldrums of the spirit, shrouded for months on end in a mist
nothing can penetrate, no messages get through, nothing
to comfort or bring relief – how even a tree
can survive there, frayed and reckless and utterly bare,
offering no shade, no fruit worth eating, how it draws its sap
from stone, is a mystery past knowing. But it does;
and sometimes there's an ageless, nameless couple there
who eat pickles by the jar and salted herring,
continually repaint the walls to match our restlessness,
play bezique all night with our diminishing pack of cards
until they've lost them all and there's nothing left for anyone to do
but wait for the sun to come out. No wonder they say

I could go mad in a place like that – besides,
what do I know about fishing? Only the lure
of its skills: patience and cunning; the arcane lore
of tackle and rod, unravelling knots in a tangled net;
the practice of solitude and the sly kinship with fish
that grows in the blood, like desire – a sweetness,
a spreading warmth – urgent as evolution
on this bleak, eroded headland where the wind, and the sea
tumbling on rocks, never hesitate one moment.

THE ARABIAN BIRD

[...] forty days journey; and in all this way there is scarce any
green thing to be met with, nor beast nor fowl to be seen or heard;
nothing but sand and stones, excepting one place which we passed
through by night; I suppose it was a village, where were some trees,
and, we thought, gardens.
— *The Pilgrimage of Joseph Pitts to Meccah and Medina,* 1680

Blistered and parched, days past count
we had travelled since then: I remembered
nothing, there was nothing to remember here
or feel, a tomb it was and the sun
bled us dry and blind as the stones.

Until, that night, hearing a sound
as of men talking in the other room,
I catch a voice but not its words

but this not a voice, though a shrill
trembling of the black acacias
spoke then of gardens,
a green-tiled town, and of the lap of water
in the fountain court, like lips I've known.

Then the wound opened, bled freely
and a startled bird took flight.
I felt the heat and the gust of its wing.

CAIRO NIGHTCLUB

As the voices slur her accent comes distinct,
the Texan heiress with the Lebanese, the exiled rich.
We are watching dwarves and juggling children,
a dancer's thighs in the harsh red light, and when
the girls are bought and our company half-gone
a boy comes on, he's pale as dawn, flashing his body
to her heavy eyes – Veronique, ageing and blonde,
declines into sleep, a temporary refuge.

For the war goes on, we take it for granted,
we all have our dead. The Lebanese jockey,
the small aggressive one, says at the Beirut racetrack
the horses went berserk. 'They ran around,
bashing their heads against trees, killing themselves.'

1977

SHY MOUNTAIN CHILDREN

One, another, then two more appear
and disappear behind the rocks – it's their flash
and sparkle gives them away, the sudden shine
of eyes and teeth and flowing hair, as they flit
like birds beside the path.

They must have followed us
from the village we had passed,
the few bare, scrubbed huts of mud and straw
still as the Sabbath and nobody there
but one woman clothed in red who stared at us
from an open loft. Suppose, I thought,
suppose I had been born…

We stopped at the river and watched them come:
small, dark, alert to every sign.
One girl was boldest, gripping your scarf
and not letting go, then touching your hair
with her tiny hands. One boy stood back
and pulled a face, as if afraid
we'd vanish if he smiled, or of our want
to give them something better than we had.

She took your scarf, of course, the girl
the others followed, running barefoot
back the way we'd come. And we waded
across the shallow river and climbed the bank
to the hot, new-surfaced road. Refreshed
and exhausted by the high bright air

we fell asleep in the local bus.
I dreamt I was at home, but there was water
brilliant and cold, and children running there –
then woke to foreign voices
and the lights of an unknown town.

AFTERNOON IN NAPLES

We climbed up
through narrow, overhanging streets
the sun couldn't reach,
distracted by cooking smells

and rooms we had no access to,
cluttered with wardrobes
and giant beds, framed madonnas
and the photographs of absent relatives.

Even high up, where the rich lived
and dressed more like us, where the map
promised gardens and open spaces,
the streets abruptly turned

and blocked the view, the famous view
with everything in it, the bay
and the dead volcano and the houses
crowding the slopes, dazzling on postcards.

We came down at last
to the man who sold shellfish
from a seaside cart, with wooden sticks
to prise them out.

His little yellow lightbulbs
bobbed up and down
against the soft, wide, horizontal of the sea
like pinpricks in the dark.

WHITE RUSSIAN

Write him down, you said, the old
French gentleman we met in Paris,
the one with the labrador
and the dead White Russian wife.

She painted blood-red flowers
and pallid women with slender necks,
memorials to a remote childhood
that history had gobbled.

They hung like ikons in his room,
very cold and still. We sat
in their shadows, at a table
laid with ancient bread and cheese,

while he spoke of Anna Semonova
and of driving down to Cannes
in a white Rolls Royce. Before long
you wanted to escape that place,

his room with its curtains drawn
against the little daylight left,
so we hurriedly wrote addresses
and were free to go. The darkness

oppressed you, made darker still
by the quickness of his mind,
and an hour later in the galleries
of the outdated Musée de l'Art Moderne

it still persisted. Remember
I love you, remember it was he,
as we crossed the street from the café,
who placed himself in our hands.

TRAVELLING BACK

In a poor country, there's joy
in mere survival – arriving late, finding a room
for the night, children everywhere.

You could buy them by the hour –
but not the women, who were veiled or absent.
The man nodded, prepared to bargain.

One watched me as I ate, not for money
but to lick the empty bowl when I let it go.
I, in turn, watched him, his village

of corrugated iron and mud-brick houses
stitched to the hillside, its single winding street
like a nursery rhyme I knew by heart.

MORNING POEM

Now is sunlight on our table
on coffee cooling in chipped blue mugs,
your hair too and your eyes reflect
this invasion of light.

You are a child in Italy
breakfasting with your father I'll never meet,
while slowly across the lake
the night fishing boats return.

THE CROSSING KEEPER

A depression moving southwards
crosses the railway line at exactly the moment
the car arrives at the end of a line
of cars, bicycles, impatient to get through.

The engine shudders to a halt
to a jangle of keys. It's all electric now,
lights flashing and a flimsy bar
across my half of the road: the other half leads back.

The ashtray is full to choking. Cows
doze in the field, an abandoned combine harvester
gathers dust till Monday: it's on days like this
I'd get hay fever, have to lie indoors

red-eyed and puffy, while sunlight
flickered through curtains and the air brimmed
with the voices of guests, having tea
and ice cream in the garden outside.

Their conversation drifted
like a stray cloud, impossibly remote, their laughter
is a butterfly skimming the poppies
in hardly a breath of wind.

And almost before you've noticed it
a sealed train has approached
without even a whistle and is already gone.
It leaves an exaggerated silence

the old crossing keeper enters, dragging the gate
back across the lines, then cupping
his hands to relight his pipe –
seeing a matchbox there on the verge.

THE VILLAGER'S TALE

There was a storm once
is unlikely to be forgotten, now the guidebooks
elaborate with scholarly detail
the marvellous frescoes that were destroyed.

Skilled hand and visionary eye
were one, they claim, in the execution of belief
on a bare wall: not
that we recognised that, simply the shock

of seeing ourselves up there
as saints and demons, and they among us
ploughing our fields, or idling on the green
by the bridge, our meeting place.

On the night of the storm I lay with Mary
in the tithe barn by the river.
She was drowned in the flood, the flood
took everything…There, now, the date

and the highest level the water reached –
but she was too far out to reach,
no one could have saved her
or that image of her, her perfect likeness –

are marked on the wall where the youngsters sit
kicking their heels, ogling the girls
out of school and the tourists' foreign cars.
The barn was declared unsafe

and pulled down, also that house
where the idiot child was locked, so long
we forgot he was there – but remember
him often now, his quiet knocking.

CHELSEA
(from Butler's Wharf*)*

Among Turner's last drawings are those he did
of a drowned prostitute, hauled out of the river
along the Chelsea embankment. He was living then
as Captain Booth, the retired seadog agreeably settled
by his waterside haunts – and haunted still,
transparently, by a terrible sun belaying its light
on flesh as canvas. See him there
on the steps, that gruff, obstreperous man confused
and empowered by the mixing of identities, working
and working his lines, trying to get her figure right.

Before they take her away. Take her away. But this
he could never flatter, the human figure
in its singular form, the ways its contours incline
from their strict latitude. Napoleon himself diminished
almost to vanishing point, a frazzled stump
between *walls* of flame… Heads down or turned away
from the surge of light, his cowering
matchstick armies and fishermen digging for bait
might be marking their cards or checking the time –
a dog was easier, at least its howl made sense.

AMNESTY

Envelopes would arrive containing newsletters
and circulars for distribution: atrocity stories,
photographs of missing persons, of backs and
soles of feet showing evidence of torture.

Now he works to mend people's bodies, in a white
coat in controlled temperatures under glare-free lights.
Now he's married and tries to get home
in time to read to his children before bed.

I used to think you had to know the names of all
wild flowers and birds, etc., to be a poet.
There's Edward Thomas still stomping his dogberry
lane, and there's acrid gunsmoke withering the air.

A TOUR OF THE HOLY LAND

In this city, the taxi drivers have a grim sense of humour
and drive too fast. They look at you, not the road,
in the rear-view mirror. They tell you their woes
in lurid, neon tones, sparing nobody, and expect yours
to be at least as bad. They wind down the window
to spit out phlegm and cigar butts and to shout at girls,
but you are already two blocks way before you can put a name
to the face of the one who, waiting to cross, has tied your heart
in a knot.
            Amanda. Miranda. Their names are the names of streets
that lead unerringly to an angle of shadow
on the Indian bedspread, or a small bottle containing bluish liquid
rolling along the dresser top until only the moment
keeps it from falling. Like a sultry, pouting mouth
that is about to ask for the loo but just might,
just because it is so unexpected, be about to reveal
some notorious truth – how else explain the countenance
of one who, simply by entering your field of vision,
excites your interest? But you cannot just barge across
and ask for the meaning of life on a plate, because the big words
are timid, are terrified of zoos, they have gone into hiding
somewhere between the library books and the worry about supper
and feeding the plants... 'Have you ever,' one asks,
'been here before?' And so the game of hunt-the-thimble begins
without benefit even of names, for the host is not formal.

No wonder the tourists have to check their map
at every corner. A sullen wind almost tears it from them
but they have high hopes of the alleyways tucked in behind,
the markets you could stroll in on weekday afternoons
when there's nothing on TV, when the weather is better

than it has been these past years… The Gateway to Adventure
is not a ruined inn where Columbus slept but a cracked
gutter or a pool of oily rainwater or the sight
of a restaurant fascia that sets your memory reeling backwards
from the shock of recognition: and no time is allowed
to adjust the focus and snap the shutter, for the city
is in the throes of major reconstruction.
                                            The farmlands
are receding, the milk churn a pinprick of light
that continues to glow, faintly, after the current
has been switched off. It seems only yesterday you phoned
from that kiosk, yet children have grown to adults
in the night between. Even the cathedral is sinking
by so many inches per year into the mire, terminal mites
are eating its heart out – and when the pumping
machines have stopped and the last phalanx of scaffolding
has been dismantled, what will greet us, then, in the proverbial
light of dawn? Or when, years later, the taxi drops you
at the block where she lived? Not, surely, the object of faith,
though the stained-glass windows may retain at least some
of the original blue… The driver says something
you don't catch, or something so extraordinary
you must have misheard. It's too early to say. You count the change
and enter the lobby. The lift is a tiny cage – almost you forget
which button to press, see hers with another's initials
scratched on the panelling, begin to wonder
whether it's all been a terrible mistake. Other versions
have the bottle empty and not rolling but thrown; it broke
and you cut your hands, but that too may be a childhood incident
you have been told of so often you have come to believe in.

After lunch, the all-party committee resumes its discussion
of what is to be built on the waste ground
behind the new flats: an opera house? A miniature
golf course (*polite laughter*)? Or a multi-storey car park
with underground ice rink? This last
seems a foregone conclusion, but the agenda gets lost
in a fog of digression; and although the flats
are no longer new and although a whole unseen generation
is already dividing into opposed minorities,
each with its book of rights, there is always someone
who insists on the need for a tight-lipped, even
for a glamorous secretary to take minutes in laborious shorthand
when all our jokes and hesitations
might be instantly and indelibly recorded on cassette.

The light thickens, darkens, and the streets
are unnaturally quiet. The chairman remembers the Thirties
through a haze of stale cigar smoke: newsreels,
cinema queues, the last tram home and the lamp-lit face
of a girl from the north... No one doubts the waste.

> Everywhere in the interior it is taken as a natural occurrence that
> the ghosts of the dead walk for a time after death.
> – Lt.-Col. P. H. Fawcett, *Exploration Fawcett*

Seven years after Colonel Fawcett vanished
in his last attempt to find the fabled pre-Inca cities,
a Swiss trapper encountered a man he believed
to be Fawcett...

                         In '56 my father died.
I was almost an orphan – half guilty, half elated.
At school, saying he'd been killed in the war
made the situation somehow normal:
everyone else had a father, death
occurred only in the films
we watched on Wednesdays after tea instead of prep.

And there was always the chance he'd come back,
just see what we'd been up to.

                *

Dated 1954, a letter to my aunt
from the British Field Sports Society (Scotland)
marks the page on which a man dies of shock
when his wife is bought back from the Indians
with her four children, for £300.

And the lady of Riberalta who from time to time
went off alone into the forest
to live with Pacaguaras Indians:
'Her collection of tooth necklaces and other
savage curios was unequalled.'

Each chapter leads off with a comic-book vignette:
a giant tarantula
on its victim's naked chest, a man overboard
being rapidly devoured by piranhas.
All that is left is the head above water.

BLUES AND AFTER

Monday, washday. I wanted my jeans
to be faded like the others were. I sweated
in a scalding bath to get them skin-tight.

They had listening booths in the record shops then.
I asked for the names I'd heard.
I joined up the dots on the pegboard walls...

On my second-hand sky-blue bike
I disappeared for weeks – using side roads only,
sleeping rough in barns, as if in hiding.

I hated myself
in shop windows. I liked – but never said so –
the barber's shop, its background array

of pin-ups and Durex, its foreground small talk
of football and money and work, while the scissors
fussed at the edges...

I moved out, found a room I called a garret.
Sunday lunchtimes, I'd hear my landlady come up
then quietly knock: meat mashed potatoes, tinned peas.

Later, I married a foreign girl
who made me wear baggy cords, like not just her idea
of an English country gentleman.

CYCLING IN LINCOLNSHIRE

There's my bicycle standing
under a dripping tree, open country
behind and the rain coming down
in silver spokes...

You could believe the earth was flat,
bounded by a sea with a Latin name.
Wild man Tennyson
scuttled along the hedgerows

leaving a trail of damp red herrings:
birdsong, and the insistent jingle
of an ice-cream touting for custom
in the New Town estates.

Once, staying bed and breakfast
in the middle of nowhere, I shared a room
with a Chinese mature student
who took his presence there for granted.

I preferred sleeping rough in barns.
Sometimes, the farmer's wife
would bring me hot milk
and would stand in the open doorway
watching me drink it too fast –

        Next morning,
I'd leave at dawn: a keen recruit
in the resistance movement.

THE COUNTRY HOUSE

No one ever claimed the room was soundproof.
You lie awake, unbelieving. Every scuffling noise,
every footstep that might not be a footstep
brings its trial of innuendos
to be resisted. The heat becomes unbearable
and at 3 a.m. a girl finds her way to the kitchen
for her rendezvous with the perfect listener.

After tea and a slice of cold ham
she reads the leaves in your cup: doom, disaster,
then sudden rescue at the eleventh hour. How anyone
can take this seriously, you cannot begin
to understand. You imagine that plopping noise
might be over-ripe apples, as if the house you are in
were in some 1920s highbrow novel.

The distance, measured in aeons, is fractional.
But tomorrow when you meet her by chance
at the turnstile, she'll reel off a list of names
not one of which you recognise. Sounds
like metallic thunder take over the air
and this, she says, is only the warm-up band
plucking a few chords, testing the microphones.

IBRAHIM STREET

Volvos imported by flying carpet
seethe between mountains of garlic, okra, dwarf onions,
explosive tomatoes and Siamese carrots –

1950s baby Austins
nudge the wheels of fortune, the creaking man-size wheels
of perilous carts drawn by donkeys or horses

as a child would draw them, the crude
simplicity of it
shot through with axles and bolts –

Boys on tinpot bicycles wearing trays of hot loaves
weave, pirouette and cadenza
an elaborate flowing script

through a cast of thousands, timeless oriental
extras in torrid epics,
gap-toothed, hobble-legged, with filmy trachoma eyes

who'll abruptly emit a guttural spray
like an ambush of blunted scimitar blades
at noon in the defile –

And the women buying and selling, women at women's work
which is most of the work of this world, women
who turn the wheels, who drag the carts,

who catch just a glimpse of in-between time
flashing by in an instant, their narrow eyes
through their black veils

stained with mustard-seed and cinnamon and tears.

ARAB WOMEN

Passing in a taxi
building-site labourers
carrying baskets of earth from a pit:
how beautiful
are the daughters of the poor.

A certain age...
In two or three years
she'll be called for as arranged
by some idiot from the south
who has the money to pay for a new roof.

The president's wife
reeking of perfume, at a charity opening
makes a sly joke
about liberation
for the benefit of the foreign press.

The married ones, those
who can afford convention,
wade into the sea
no deeper than their breasts
still wearing all their clothes.

CATACOMBS

These 'extensive underground galleries'
built to house the tombs of Christians
who died in the Roman games –

Stepping down between the damp walls
she cannot bring herself to touch,
she can go no further...

In daylight again and feeling the heat,
she potters around the village –
children and chickens, a sheep's head
still dripping blood – as if this
were home, as if she'd locked herself out
and her husband was on his way.

Once, and once only, she left him alone
to visit her sister.
He took off his watch,
brought water to the boil,
then cooked it for three and a half minutes.

HOW DID YOU GET ABOUT?

The grimy ticket-office window,
its waist-high opening
a funnel for hands and voices
placing bets on available seats.

The enormous man behind
who has all the time in the world
to discuss the pros and cons
but closes on the dot.

The timetable board
showing departures to the nearest hour
like the board in an English church
announcing hymns.

Grave mechanics
in attitudes of passive resistance
who'll abruptly assault a wheel
in a hammering rage.

Old men with their several women
and neatly tied bundles
immobile, immune,
past all expectation.

Bored teenage soldiers
with their cheeks against their rifles
and their mouths wide open
scratching their crotches.

A child pissing
in a puddle of dusty oil,
a wayward trickle
going mostly down his legs.

Babies sleeping or suckling
while flies about their faces
move terribly close
to their lips and eyes.

In short, by bus. Battered
but still untamed, jabbering clouds
of dense exhaust, it jolts
through a six-point turn

then out to sudden brightness,
the heat, the sun drumming down
and a voice wailing of love
from a tinny transistor.

REPRISALS

Each night around 10 o'clock someone goes out
to hose down the terrace. There's the scuff
and slap of his sandals –

These grand hotels are headed nowhere,
ocean liners with working parts...
My lone companion, a primary school teacher
back after 20 years
to a house in ruins and a single uncle,
says tourism is to blame
for the decline in the local fishing industry,
says politics are to blame
for the lack of tourists.

His children are designing a new flag...
We are eating grapes and watching the new moon
and remembering what it was like:
cocktails and jazz piano,
the women in extravagant gowns and the men
in colonial whites – though we are neither
old enough to have been there.

Then I tell him about the programme
I saw last year: how the dog-handlers
got a guinea for every one bitten
and a cup for every dead Arab.
For a while it's so quiet between us
we can hear moths buffeting the light.

Next morning in Karachi
there's a ragged guard of honour,
a line of assorted footwear
in the airport lounge, waiting to be claimed.

ANNIGONI

My director has only minutes to spare.
He's fine, his children are fine, his institute prospers.
He has put on weight
and grown even smaller. There are students waiting.

Days to the south, conscript soldiers
do their best to keep out of the enemy's sights
in a landscape without natural cover...
The ashtrays might never have been emptied.

For a year here I taught the rudiments
of the English language; Annigoni's Queen
and a photo Hassan Deux in dapper lounge suit
graced the classroom walls. Mornings

were housewives – and one, I recall, for the national holiday,
was flying to London. Our vocabulary lesson
was designed around what she should pack:
toothbrush, hairbrush, passport, visa, umbrella.

After the freak storms the river is swollen
and brown, the bidonville alleys ankle-deep in mud.
Kites and the tourist charter planes seem reluctant to land.
On the ornate façade the masonry is loose, and those

who step out on the balcony with a glass of wine
and a favoured companion, or simply to watch
the girls in Paris dresses stroll the Boulevard
Libération, do so at their own risk.

THE HOLIDAY ALBUM

1 *A Meeting*

My friend... So soon on first-name terms, so soon
our language lessons enable us to call
what lies between us salt, pepper, bottle of wine
or empty bottle. Sunlight's a feast
to eyes starved of the strong simplicities
of sea, sky, the cut-throat edge of whitewashed walls
against the blue: I'm like a child again, hungry
for knowledge I'll never forget, these very words
spelt out on the tablecloth the waiter
is about to whisk off – and with such dash,
such sleight of hand and modest eyes as become
a conjuror hired for the lull after feeding,
a true professional who leaves everything just
as he found it, and our looks of incomprehension.

2 *A Preference*

I like ports best, for the bundles of money
exchanged through car windows, beneath statues of admirals;
for the girls at corners in fishnet tights
and the sailors on leave from Gilbert & Sullivan;
for the stalls selling luminous dolls, cheap cigarettes
and whisky, Taiwan transistors and plastic madonnas
in waves of silk scarves, all fallen
off the back of a boat. For the Vespas revving at night
in narrow streets. For the halting funicular ride
to a classier district: bored matrons
adrift on tiny balconies. Trees tactfully placed

to give a sense of scale. A dog-eared park from where,
for a coin plugged in a stubby telescope, you can see
the Fortunate Isles, only a day-trip away.

3   *A List*

What we have not got to see: the chapel of San Jeronimo
(there being so many Jeronimos, and so many of these
having met their ends in bizarre martyrdoms,
the details of which the guidebooks lovingly dwell on;
and the others, simple hermits who turn a blind eye
like the man in room 203 with his affable
greetings, whatever the weather or temper we're in).
The frescoes in the said chapel, dubiously restored.
The view across the bay, of which the postcards say it all,
and the private collection of torture instruments.
The tomb of the unknown warrior, dedicated to a god
equally unknowable, and the four horses that have waited
so long, while the ambassadors also are waiting to see
how their gifts are received, they have turned to stone.

4   *A Dream*

I dreamt we'd gone hunting, having set out early
to catch the dawn; and though clumsy,
unpractised with guns, blood oozed from my sack,
from my bulging pockets that slowed me down
as something quickened: leaves twitching, a scent,
a flicker of light in a rock's shadow, a glimpse

of old Adam who whispered to use both... Today,
from my window above the yard, as my tongue
seeks a way round these obstinate clusters of consonants
you pronounce for me laughing, with that gargle
at the back of your throat that can seem, repeated
with insistence, a sexual affront, I count seven
separate species: cats, dogs, donkeys, pigs, hens,
a goat, a rat, besides the insects and birdlife.

5   *An Invitation*

And you: 'Come, I want to show you views
of the inner lives of burghers, of the glistening
barbs of rush-hour traffic; of the tall rooms
light's woven into through slatted shades
in the long siesta hour; of the high-rise office blocks
beaming transcendence out of all proportion to our
weekday afternoon errands, and of the blood-orange glow
at sunset like a withdrawing note of farewell
that permeates our fixtures, the squat colonnades and statuary
that adorn the central station; of the dark
hollows of churches, underwater sensation of looking up
through mottled brightness, where each syllable drops
like a worn penny in the collection box and the font
of baptism's crusted with an echo at its rim.'

BEADS, WHIPS AND AMULETS

You are writing a commentary on his work.
You have this idea there may be some early drafts about
and you know the apartment block where his last
mistress lives with her engineer husband.

How she must hate the graduate students
with their prepared questions!
This is where the poet came to forget:
boats, a few bars, a backward economy –

where businessmen from the north now come
for weekends, where trim yachts
stay moored all summer and beside the marina
North African vendors set out their identical wares.

Among the bestsellers you were lucky to find
his book in translation. You laze
on the stony beach with the middle-aged German women,
turning down the corners of pages...

Every day towards five o'clock the vendors
pack up their kitbags and move off,
blending with nightfall. Tourist information
has found you a cheap hotel but you can't sleep

for the disco noise and the scooters: just as
years ago his poems kept you awake,
reading through to dawn by a 40-watt bulb
while the goods trains shunted and clattered.

One night, a man comes to your door complaining bitterly.
You offer him money, shutting him out, and his stick
taps away down the stairs. There's a dry
rustle of grasses, and the sound of waves pressing in.

TIMUR THE LAME

A man with a limp came towards me,
begging money for liquor – spoke of cairns
built of skulls, of the wind off the steppes
on the night before battle
and the evils of cholesterol.

Some of this, I thought, he must be making up.
Besides, what was I doing here,
talking with a dead Mongol warrior
in the middle of the life that was mine?

At the end of the street, some camels
grazing, the air mottled with flies
above ribbons of goat flesh...
Even the tourists looked sick.
Even the women, that day, were not untouched.

He said: You think a life
has a beginning, middle and end?
Then he emptied his pockets
and showed me the eyes of Hafiz.

ARLINGTON MANSIONS

Towards midnight on my thirtieth birthday
I was teasing a 5-amp fuse wire
between a pair of recalcitrant screws,
remembering in the dark
April 12, 1961: Yuri Gagarin, first man alive
to see the whole blue ball in space,
and myself aged ten in the back of a car
being driven east.

A dog came scratching for food.
A bowl of cold chicken curry later,
I half-led, half-pushed it back home
to the gaga lady upstairs –
the Flower Girl, the Millionairess,
former star of the silent screen –
who lived on chocolate and cigarettes.

Sshhh, she whispered, one finger on her lips,
the same sound of the sea
I could hear beyond Flamborough Head.

FROG PRINCE

Am I good or bad, clever or stupid?
Stendhal asks himself
in the summer of 1832.

A life of falling in love and off horses...
Carriage wheels on cobbles, a rattle
of distant muskets: it's half past one

in the morning and already too hot to think
or sleep, yet eleven hundred pretty women a year –
he has seen the official statistics –

leaving the ballrooms of Paris at dawn
are catching colds from which they die.
Meanwhile the Duke of Frioul

at the age of thirty-eight – 'the age when,'
as Stendhal himself remarks, 'if one is disillusioned,
boredom begins to appear on the horizon' –

is strolling about, alone and slightly drunk,
in the gloom of the Palais Royal gardens,
where a boy is catching frogs

for the knife of Dr Edwards, an Englishman,
who seeks a cure for the women's complaint
and to discover how we breathe.

KRONSVERSKAYA PROSPEKT

One week there is nothing but apples,
the next week herring
and the next cabbages, most of them already rotten.

Anna brings home the cabbages
and makes a stew for ten or a dozen people.
Then they talk into the night
about the masterpieces of world literature
they are even now translating,
the plays they will put on
and how the shapes of even spoons and forks
will be changed by the new perspective.

Moura and Mariussa are standing by the window.
What Moura's caught sight of
is a house in the country with running water
where people she doesn't know
are eating meat and fresh bread – then a cloud
scuds across the moon.

Mariussa who is the youngest of all
and will be the last to die, if allowed to live out
the span of his natural life, Mariussa too
is still hungry, he is tracing his own disappearance –
eyes, hair, nose lips –
with his finger on the wet pane.

THE CHESS PLAYER

I'm thinking of a famous grandmaster
on the sixteenth floor of a hotel in Bucharest
kept awake by the gypsy music
of a wedding party downstairs.

I'm seeing him watch from his window
some cleaning women emerge
in the sodium-lit small hours
from the national exhibition centre,
and the rails from the station stretching
towards the vanishing point of asylum.

When at last he falls asleep
to the strains of the last violin
he dreams fitfully
of a lady with a parasol
stepping out on the first marble square
of a black-and-white chequered piazza.

His task is to guide her across
to the shade of the colonnade
before history takes over,
before the city lies in ruins.

The light is hot and even
and, like the Pyramids when they were built,
the stones are so perfectly cut
a knife blade couldn't slip between them.

1988

When they entered the private apartments
they found wall-to-wall wardrobes of Paris clothes
and a room made into a cinema
for watching favourite American films.

Caesar also, with Calpurnia,
no doubt whiled winter evenings away
with wine, musicians and foreign dancers
as I too enjoy American films… Soldiers
lined up in a square, a crowd of civilians –
then someone gives the order, and they fire.

Later, scenes of public rejoicing
as the border is opened…
Meanwhile, a man we have learnt to care about
is searching among the fallen
for a young girl – there is always a subplot
with a young and beautiful girl.

She lives alone in a block of flats.
Her brother has been killed.
It is evening and the electricity has been cut off
and she is writing fast: 'I want to tell you
about that church behind the stadium,
when they unlocked the door…'

Here I see her pause and look up,
glancing over her shoulder
as if there were someone else in the room.
But there is no one, it is only a noise in the street.

I DIDN'T MEAN TO KILL MY HUSBAND

she said, and I believed her, as we came out of Finnegan's
at nine o'clock on a rainy evening
and headed for somewhere to eat. Water was running
down the roofs and gutters
like the Nile in flood, and when she closed her blue, blue eyes
when we kissed,
I knew she was the kind of person
who just lets what will happen happen, as I was too.

CARTOGRAPHY

Miles back, we had taken a wrong turning.
Fields, fields without sheep or cattle, and the oncoming traffic
repeated themselves in a continuous loop
and I thought perhaps you were sulking but no,
you said, just thinking, wondering in fact
where that passage in Lawrence was
about nothing being left in the world
except himself and a rabbit – was it in *Apocalypse*
or the Penguin selection from *Phoenix*?

Rain was spotting the windscreen, not enough for the wipers,
and your small rounded toes
where you'd kicked off your shoes
under what I still called the glove compartment
were clenching then more slowly unclenching...
We were headed towards some infamous inn
in the middle of nowhere – until a warning sign,
ESTATE FARM SHOP 200 YARDS, and I slowed
and then parked on the gravel outside.

Tea towels and pottery mugs and recipe books
in what had once been a barn, now lit
with fluorescent bulbs. In-laws, you said,
or wicked stepmothers, is who this stuff is for.
A freezer held packs of fish and game
'flown in yesterday from Scotland', according to the girl
when she'd turned down her Walkman. And opening
the lid, I felt the chill of Mercator: the globe
sliced open and ruled, splayed on a cut-and-dried page.

LION CUB

Lost in the garden suburbs, where the sprinklers
swung idly on lawns and the bored, incurious sentries
with loaded carbines

regarded us passing: two men and one girl
out on the town… Raising the spirit
of competition.

There were all-night bars
where the players and dancers from the nightclubs around
came to drink between sessions

with the second sons of the newly rich;
car chases along the Corniche,
swimming nude in the Sporting Club pool;

a diminishing row of clay cups
on the table before me, in the hashish parlour
I never found again in daylight.

The bouncers
who had us leave the nightclub
where we emptied the floor by dancing à trois –

and the casino at the Sheraton,
and the private apartment in Zamalek
where the lion cub went missing –

worked as a team, polite but strict
as the parents of an only child
who is going to get somewhere in life.

CANARIES

I was in love that summer – it is worth a summer
to be young and in love
in a foreign city.

Everything was rounded and just touching
like the curves in the wrought-iron grille
above my apartment door.
I thought: there may be something more to life
than this, but not much more.

Walking home in the late afternoon
down a street of workshops, mechanics' dens, stray dogs
and sometimes sheep, as I neared the shop
that sold caged birds
I'd shut my eyes – to hear
as if underground the canaries singing.

EXPAT

An address I can't pronounce, a divan,
a teach-yourself Arabic, a draft
of his time-and-motion report and a girl named Susan
arrived from the airport with whisky and cornflakes.

One night, after too much drinking,
she gets up at dawn for a pee
and sees or dreams through the bathroom window
a sheep being killed by two men.

It's some festival, she thinks.

It's some festival, he tells her
over the cornflakes. They've been invited
by a neighbour, a man high up in the national bank,
to break the fast with his family.

Something yellow goes by in the street...
There are people they both know still mowing the lawn
and walking the dog; wives, mortgages
in the middle distance, an enormous sum.

FROM A 94 BUS

The children of the rich are girls aged four or five
riding the backs of cars with fast acceleration
should the need arise which it rarely does.
Tied loosely round their necks are straw or felt hats with ribbons.

Their teeth and skin and hair are without blemish.
Their tantrums are the stuff of legend, ditto their *sang froid*.
Without ever having spoken to them or come within earshot
battalions have died with these girls' names on their lips.

Already they know everything there is to be known about money and sex
and they know that they know it. In the crooks of their little fingers
is written the history of their class and whether their brothers
prosper or go to the dogs makes no difference at all.

Wherever they will arrive they will be expected.

THE OFFICE SUITE

1 *Bifocals*

He asked if I'd had a good journey
and how I saw myself in ten years' time.

Balding, bifocals, his name
and title stencilled on the door –
I was supposed to look him straight back
and say: 'Sitting where you are now.'

What were the long-term prospects
for literature in the video age?
And how, we wondered,
had our single mutual acquaintance
made such a mess of his brilliant future?
… Staring the while
at the brick wall opposite
where the rain gave itself away
in splinters of light.

I couldn't do it… I recalled
a man on the Underground
of about my own age
methodically tearing an advert for mouthwash
into smaller and smaller pieces.

Depilatory cream and pregnancy testing
would be the next to go.
I'd committed their texts to heart
rather than meet his eyes.

2 *Johnson*

He kept calling the librarian
by the name of the one
before the one she'd replaced.

And sometimes in mid-afternoon, returning
from the Taj Mahal or the Café Venezia,
he stepped out of the lift
on the wrong floor.

Someone would have to lead him back
to his own desk, where he'd regret
not having crossed Iran
when the borders were open.

     *

Three hours into the Christmas party
he was found in reception, talking
with the night security guard
about the politics of underdevelopment.

Come on up, someone said, the fun's just beginning.
No, he replied, all that's for you youngsters –
synchronising his exit
through the revolving doors

with the entry of a Japanese tourist
who won first prize in the raffle:
a hostess trolley.

3 *Writ in Water*

Across from our office was another
like ours, but whose whole façade
was made of glass. No pane was
exactly true, and on clear mornings our late
arrivals, hangovers, feet
on desks and industrious moments
were reflected there as if in water.

Later, when they switched on their lights,
the glass gave way
like the front of an old dolls' house.
There were the serious men in suits
and the secretaries at their keyboards
and the man who clears memos from out-trays
to redistribute in in-trays.

A vent at the top uttered steam and,
one day in early spring, a brimming froth of suds
which the lightest breeze creamed off.

4 *Chronicle*

In the Year of the Ape, 1404,
for a single night
all bans were cancelled, everything was licensed.
All the dancing girls of Asia.

I remember the face of the new office temp
as she looked towards me
then back to her VDU – a face so blank, so wrapped
in the ghost noise of her Walkman,

I might equally have been her boyfriend
or Tamburlaine the Great
before he died of exhaustion
en route to China.

5 *The Whites of Their Eyes*

Count Corner at Borodino, at 4 p.m.
on 7 September 1812:
'Is this damn battle never going to finish?'
40,000 Russians and 30,000 Frenchmen
lay dead or dying around him…

So it is these weekday afternoons –
feeling drowsy and the same time restless,
wanting this thing to be over –
when Johnson comes in and gives me a look.

Up on the roof for a smoke, here's London
on parade: a race of small-boned people
threading through the eyes of streets,
stitching their lives into place.

Blink, and it's Moscow in flames –
and there's Johnson and me
up to our knees in snow
on the winter retreat.

6 *The Wine-Dark Excursion*

Discos, air-conditioned tavernas, a patch of scrub land
with goats, between half-built motels...
But the wine was good, and the brandy,
and somewhere they stopped at a garage
with a single petrol pump
and a mechanic who washed their windscreen –

A small town in the foothills
where the men marry the girls next door
and on the whole stay faithful,
bringing up their families
to a life that is not that different
from how it was, when they were children.

'A bunch of wankers,' commented Marketing,
whose English was near-perfect,
as he opened another bottle. One of the Sales girls
had fallen asleep, her friend
had begun to cry. So Accounts took the wheel
and steered them back home, or a place not too unlike,

where tomorrow they would sit in rows
in a curtained room
while a projector breamed record profits
and the Chairman thanked them all for a job well done.

CRAWLEY WELCOMES CAREFUL DRIVERS

I'd have lived opposite the Esso garage, where they put
the tiger in your tank. I'd have had three aunts –
Alice, Joan and the other one, who married beneath her –
a Hornby train set, a yoyo, a tree house, a military badge.

An only child, I'd have been allowed to stay up to watch the news.
Sometimes I would have wondered if my parents were really
my parents, and would have imagined sailing to Rio
to find my true father and meeting him in the stock exchange,

easily the tallest man there. Until then, I'd have fished
for sticklebacks with Jeremy, my friend. *His* father, something
in insurance, would have smoked a pipe with a curvy stem.
And one night, having talked about it for weeks, Jeremy

would have gone and done it: next morning, the assistant pro
would have found the bank manager's Jaguar crashed into a tree
off the eighteenth fairway and, lying on the back seat, asleep,
apparently unharmed, the bank manager's lovely naked daughter.

Around that time, I'd have opted for geography and economics.
I'd have worried about God and checked every nook and cranny for signs
of hereditary disease. Jeremy would have gone up to Oxford.
I'd have learnt how to foxtrot with his younger sister.

A SWISH OF ORGANZA

After the war, what was to be done
was to build the world anew
for the children that kept getting born.

Labour, then the fruits of labour…
Then the children shut their bedroom doors
and began to 'experiment'.

Each summer, my uncle and aunt took to water,
a cruise in the Med
where they dressed for dinner
and stopped off at the ancient ports,
returning with souvenirs.

There was dancing, and there were tables for bridge.
One night, a stranger asked if they'd mind
if he drew up a chair and watched.
When my aunt retired to bed
he was asked to make a fourth.

I imagine my uncle's serious look
across the green baize, waiting for his partner's bid
as the ship holds steady on course.
An Englishman's code: things hinted
and understood, cards played close to the chest.

The stranger was Mantovani,
Now they are alone in the bar, and Mantovani explains
how he sold his first million,
how he invented the cascading strings.
Then back to the hotel days –
success isn't cheaply bought, he says;
though luck plays a part, and chancing the odds,
it comes down in the end to hard work.

A night to remember. I think of my uncle
taking a last turn on deck, the bright
constellations above, the white of the sea spilling by.
And my aunt asleep below,
and the engines' muffled beat.

TEN MINUTES FROM THE CITY

We start at the top: the master bedroom
with en suite bathroom. And with, by the bed,
a gleaming chrome exercise machine
on which a man is cycling
down a sandy path
towards a hut made of reeds and mud...

In the smallest bedroom a child is asleep.
In the kitchen, Elke, the Dutch au pair, is reading
the evening paper and smoking Gauloises.
She is waiting for the telephone to ring.
There's a smell of burning, and the woman
who is showing me her life
hurries to the cooker, then she takes a cloth
to wipe up the mess
in which the twins, her older children, have sat.

They need more space, she says.
They are moving to the country.
They are open to offers – I must talk
with her husband, who should be home any minute.

I keep thinking about that hut, the sound
that comes from inside, and the man not getting nearer
however hard he pedals... He's there
again, sitting across the table where a dinner party
is in full swing – late forties,
tired, pouring a glass of red wine.

He is explaining the domino theory.
He clears a space among the dishes
and stands three books upright,
about three inches apart.
Then he pushes the nearest book
with his finger, and they all fall down.

So clearly do I imagine this
I can read the spines of the books… His children,
now in their teens, have seen it all before.

EARLY PHOTOGRAPHS

In the nineteenth, surely the saddest century yet,
I was a boy standing alone and very still
in the corridor of a gothic institution
of the type built to house poor orphans or the mad.

I was Darwin in Galapagos
riding a tortoise, on the brink of my big idea.
I was the fair-skinned man in Arabia Deserta
about whom Doughty, travelling later, heard rumours.

I was a pigtailed Chinese pirate
slamming down the railroad
across the US prairies.
I was beside myself with hope, anger, fear and exhaustion.

Suddenly, and at exactly the same time,
a bird in the grounds
makes its fatuous trill, and the boy
waggles his head very fast from side to side.

EADWEARD MUYBRIDGE

'My name is Muybridge,' said the night-time visitor,
'and I have a message for you from my wife.'
Then he fired a single shot

from a Smith & Wesson No. 2...
The women sitting, the men discussing
in low voices, the future rushing in

from left to right, then back to the left –
after Major Harry Larkyns had staggered back,
trailed blood through the house and out the back door,

Muybridge apologised to the ladies.
He lent his carriage to fetch a doctor
and sat down in the parlour with a newspaper.

I'd kill a man like that myself if I had to.
Sleep some hours in the afternoon, take a shower
and a gun and do it. And afterwards

– acquitted, on the grounds of Larkyns
having got his deserts – continue my experiment
involving horses, birds, male and female nudes, children

from the Blockley Hospital for the Poor,
trip wires and batteries of cameras
with shutter speeds of 1/1000th of a second.

MONDAY

My life accused me: paleface, it said, I deserve better.
Is this or is this not an advanced post-industrial democracy?

Useless explaining the menopause, or that one child in three
is born below the poverty line.

We sallied down to the leisure centre.
What are these grey bits, it asked, in my seafood salad?

THE MIRACLE AT SHEPHERD'S BUSH

By late afternoon you are standing at the barriers
around a patch of scorched grass, a piece of white clothing,
one shoe, a kite in a tree. The women with armbands

are saying nothing, only that no one
has been hurt or arrested. There's a faint smell of burning,
a lingering pink over Acton

that seems reluctant to call it a day. The choir
of the Pentecostal Church sings unaccompanied gospel hymns
and slowly you become aware just how many people

you live among are blind or dumb or are crippled
in so many ways. Some kneel and pray or weep, others light candles
on a trestle table covered with velvet or dig divots

of grass and soil which they carry off in plastic bags.
Most people are simply curious, they would like the police
or an archbishop to say for sure whether it is one thing

or another, it resembles too closely for comfort a car-boot sale
or minor demonstration against the government – except there lacks
any sense of achievement, of having stood up to be counted.

Blessed by some nuns, warned by a man with a thermos
the end of the world is nigh, you walk home past a couple
in a tent making love. Next day it is in the papers

along with a two-years-old photo of the boy with his mother
in someone's back garden, not smiling. Eye-witnesses
come forward, though you know for a fact at least two of them

were in the Coningham Arms all day. The lucrative role of father
is claimed by three. It rains, the paths worn in the green
are trodden to mud, wheelchairs get stuck, you overhear jokes

about virgin births and burning bushes. For a week,
maybe two, there are reported sightings of the mother and boy
from Stranraer, Teignmouth, Berwick-upon-Tweed,

Oslo. You think of the boy waking
to the sound of water, the morning light, his fingers
touching skin all over that must scarcely feel his own.

WISEMAN'S GRAND SUMMER CLEARANCE
i.m. T.F.

Red brick and roses, over-green lawns, a wisp of smoke
climbing a little in the airless sky,
then losing heart... After the cremation
I walked down to the high street
and stood for a long time
in front of a menswear shop: trousers,
suits and ties, three-packs of handkerchiefs,
shirts with stripes and with button-down collars –
perfectly ordinary decent clothes
that nobody wanted, not even at knock-down prices,
that seemed fated never once to be worn.

THE BIG IDEA

We were working out our redundancy notices.
We talked on the phone all morning,
looted the stationery, sat around in the canteen
thinking of ways to get rich quick:
maybe write a bestseller, maybe window cleaning
– all you needed was a bucket and ladder,
low capital investment. We emptied our desk drawers
– was this it? the sum total? – and when fire-engines
got snarled in the traffic we stood at the windows
and cheered. It was like the end of term
or the decline of the West, what we'd hardly dared
dream of seemed suddenly possible. Like Susie,
who planned to spend her pay-off on a one-way ticket
to China. She had purple lipstick
and a penthouse flat. She could hold her breath longer
than anyone I've known. We were completely
unsuited, but for the time in question love
was a thing I almost believed could filter through
to the junk yards, the scams, the base-line
of the national economy.

EX

An old girlfriend appears on TV
answering questions about the homeless.
Yes, the new government initiative
is welcome as far as it goes.
No, it doesn't even attempt
to tackle the root of the problem.

Phones are ringing behind her,
colleagues are bent over keyboards...
I want to ask how much she earns,
whether she still leaves the cap off the toothpaste
and if she has children, what are their names?

Just before we go off the air
she gives me that patient look –
as if a grasp of the basic issues
will for ever elude me,
as if I think I can make a difference
by giving money to beggars in the street
or offering them a bed for the night.

THE YEAR OF THE DOG

Bank managers, bombs in Oxford Street, buying a suit:
it was the year of starting to get serious.
Of letters of application, apology and condolence.
Of a girl sitting cross-legged on the floor
saying she would commit suicide
if she wasn't married by her twenty-fifth birthday –
she just wanted that boy–girl stuff out of the way
so she could concentrate on what was important.
Of playing for time, while admitting
that two copies of *Memories, Dreams, Reflections* in one room
were more than enough. Of knowing something
had to give, but what or who and when? One Friday
I woke up in Notting Hill with yellow greasepaint on my face:
I remember looking down from a tower-block balcony
on an empty playground and thinking it was already too late
to become a surgeon. And when the ageing whippet
I didn't even like
that belonged to the house I was house-sitting
ran off in the park, I felt my life
would never be whole again. I posted a hundred notices
on trees, railings, in local newsagents
offering a £5 reward, a lot of money then.

SWITZERLAND

Today, as it happens, there is no enemy.
– John McPhee, *The Swiss Army*

Congratulations on the new job. Helen
must be pleased, not to say relieved. Weekend use
of the company plane? Don't answer. I picture you
in one of those downtown phallic high-rises
on the postcard you sent a while back, all shiny steel
and neutral carpets, a discreet little *ping*
as you arrive on the fortieth floor, the corridors awash
with single women – and you only have to glance
at the keyboard for the national economies of half of Asia
to get the jitters (chaos theory). Then –
I can't help it – something happens, a murder, a cover-up,
a massive fraud that speaks doom to the West
as we know it. Enter the FBI. You've been framed
of course, and only the dogged devotion of this slim dark
patriotic girl in accounts can save you now…
The whole thing lasts approximately ninety minutes,
is beautiful to look at, includes a bondage scene
that's genuinely funny, and if you tap it, say,
you'd hear the sound of loose debris
falling down inside – intentional, I know… Jane
sends her love. She gets depressed. She goes shopping
in the sales, buys six pairs of boots that neither fit
nor make her look good, then feels too ashamed
to take them back. They're stacked in the bedroom
like heirlooms we can't get rid of. She says the reason
I never ask if she loves me is in case she says yes.
I don't deny it. I'm fond of her as always, never more
than when she comes back muddy and starry-eyed
from her weekend retreats, but this time

the rewind button's stuck, I think we're both in need
of a get-out clause. The weather should but doesn't help:
for weeks it's been so crisp and cold, the sky
so unbearably blue, I feel I'm living in a landlocked
neutral country where uniforms and casual wear
hang side by side in heavy wardrobes carved with griffins,
airstrips scar the forests – like someone's stuck down
Band-Aids, then peeled them off – and the mountains
are stuffed with a kind of bread that keeps for years:
a constant state of readiness for what never happens,
plus a low-level fear that the thing itself
might be mistaken for a routine practice. Altitude
sickness? Post-industrial anaemia? Do you remember that man
who used to knock on the door with his clipboard
petition, reeking of something, a kind of *ancien régime*
aftershave? Save the whales, library opening hours,
political prisoners, sleeping policemen
to cut the through traffic – I signed for everything
but in the end I got tired of playing good neighbours
and gave him the number of Madame Lynne – who for £25
tells me I can have everything I want
if I just *allow it to happen*. I haven't seen him since.

UNICORNS

A sort of dusty white, with stubby horns
that leave scaly flakes on your hands –
between the goats and donkeys
in the children's section
they are chomping their vitamin pellets.

There's a map of the world
with a few red dots, plus a text explaining
their shrinking habitat.
They don't look in danger, just tired,
or restless… And though of course

they should be returned to the wild
and set free, they appear to lack
whatever it takes, so on balance we agree
that their being where they are
is probably the right thing.

BEDTIME

holes in the sky
little monkeys peek
through the eastern gate
the street of weavers
tinsmiths alley

old woman mad as the wind
hairy scary
chasing a chicken
blood when it spills
fire-engine red

in the vizier's palace
soldiers in shakos
don't blink don't speak don't hear
people vanish
in front of their bony noses

walls have ears tables groan
heads roll
men with long white beards debate monotheism
in seven languages
no one waters the plants

will the prince on his steed
arrive in time rescue the princess
die in his bed
now the children are sleepy
they've seen enough

the knife grinder the accordion man
the night watchman with lumps on his head
bears dancing
the seller of jujubes
the chicken up and running

LISSOM

I'm sitting alone in a room
with a bandage round my head
doing nothing wrong.

Two or three times a day
a girl in her early twenties
holding a Mongol bow

comes to the open door
and looks briefly around
for the arrow.

VELCRO

> Renous, alluding to myself, asked him what he thought of the
> King of England sending out a collector to their country, to pick
> up lizards and beetles, and to break stones? The old gentleman
> thought seriously for some time, and then said… 'I do not like
> it: if one of us were to go and do such things in England, do you
> not think the King of England would very soon send us out of the
> country?'
> – Darwin, *Voyage of the Beagle*

There's a tribe, I swear it,
in the Syrian desert
who bury their dead standing up.

Every five years, a great sandstorm
rages; diviners interpret
the chattering of skulls.

*

Their warrior queen
models Armani. Their children
are force-fed videos

of the long march
out of Crittenden
to Zit. Their god is named

after the terrifying noise
made by the opening
of a hundred tent-flaps at dawn.

*

The acrid leaves they chew
every waking hour
produce a mild

hallucinatory effect
of the kind experienced
by publishers' reps

while driving on the M6
north of Carlisle
in light drizzle.

*

Because their topography
lacks high places
they have yet to invent

the ladder. Because
of the premium they place
on originality in art

no two toothbrushes, funeral masks
or wheels
are exactly the same.

*

While their diligent wives
are putting on their faces
the junior elders

assemble in the lobby
to smoke cheroots
and discuss the pros and cons

of the new technology –
franking machines, ejector seats –
over laced mint tea.

*

Lobbies, vestibules, the paths
or no man's land
between clan enclosures –

'zones of the veil'
in which a code of anonymity
is *de rigueur*,

in which nevertheless
certain covert proposals
are frequently advanced.

*

Sex: *see under* alabaster;
Earhart, Amelia; Friday.
See also tongs.

It's not that they don't
enjoy it, but are often inhibited
by their distracting need

to rationalise the gap
between the gritty norm
and their culture's pellucid ideal.

*

The present *fatir* – oracle
of the supreme being,
paraded in public

only once every forty-two years
and in times of extreme
political crisis –

is a copy dating
from the 1950s, the original
having been lost.

*

Travellers are welcome
during the feast of Gordon
but should take care to depart

before the unwonted outpouring
of intertribal affection
is bitterly regretted.

*

Small roadside cairns
mark the graves of children
hit by cars

while dashing out
in playful ambush
of foreign buyers

for beads and lucky charms
laid out in rows
on plastic sheets.

*

Dust. Boredom. An ant
buried under a handful of sand
scrabbles and blusters

its way to the surface
only to be buried again…
Each year the elders

devise yet more creative
firework displays
and evening classes.

*

A sinecure for life
is awarded annually
for the most formally elaborate

Horatian ode
that celebrates the virtues
of working women –

their hardiness
and sufferance,
their brazen knees.

*

The Mawami's pigtails
are unrelated
to the fanciful hairstyles

in the famous mezzotint
of 1821
by Thomas Hobson,

an inveterate liar
who never left
his native Lyme Regis.

*

Renowned abroad
for his charitable works
and stylish dressing,

the Mawami remains
conservative at heart –
rather than hear

bad news, he has the throats
of messengers slit
before they can speak.

*

Their champion athletes'
habitual loping gait –
acquired by years of running

through loose sand –
is much imitated
by both teenage boys

who wish to attract a mate
and girls protesting
at the restraints upon their sex.

*

The pauses
in the speech of the old –
neither shortness of breath

nor the occlusion
of memory,
but steadfast adherence

to the rules of grammar:
each word being set
in its frame of silence.

*

Lifetimes have been gladly spent
mastering just one
of their sacred texts

by scholars who still confuse
the place names and numbers
that may also serve

as intimate endearments
with those that articulate
disgust.

*

To sons departing
on government scholarships
for study abroad

mothers give pellets
of hardened camel dung
as *memento mori.*

Traces may be found
among the dust and fuzz
in their jacket pockets.

*

Booty carried home:
Levi's, Anglepoise lights,
cordless toasters;

a working knowledge
of alleles, zygotes,
stress fractures

and of the sexual preferences
of older women
in South Dakota.

*

Ever since the cataclysmic
civil war
between al-Origbi and Philip

twins have been both shunned
and revered –
for the drear month of penitence

that follows their birth,
for the good times enjoyed
by the priesthood.

*

No less than the beauty
of their sheltered daughters,
the limpid simplicity

of their myth that accounts
for the birth of the world
compels assent.

*

For that one four goats,
a Sanyo fan
and access rights

to a dubious well.
For this a green card.
And for this true love

plus a room of her own –
no girl
without her brideprice.

*

Twice a day
for seven weeks
in a chipped tin mug

a mixture of earwax,
fertiliser
and the liquor sold

by the blind widow
will guarantee exemption
from military service.

*

Cleaning the filters,
raking the dunes –
the hereditary labour

of the *doowalis*.
Bourgeois standing
is signified

by having nothing pressing to do
and a vacant expression
in the bloodshot eyes.

*

The coincidence
between the combined ages
of the Mawami's wives

and the acquisition number
inked behind the ear
of the hunting fetish

in the museum of folk art
in Aleppo
has been remarked.

*

As also the perfect circles
and figures-of-eight
described by caravans

whose raddled guides
still navigate
by the stars –

the Molars,
the Gang of Four,
the Timid One.

*

From December to March
a seasonal wind
infiltrates sand

into every orifice.
Domestic violence
and hard-core video rentals

peak, lending support
to those who argue
for stricter censorship.

*

The wind itself,
say their opponents,
is to blame.

They attack it with knives,
harpoons; or woo it
with tenderness,

hanging feathers and chimes
on the boughs of trees
to temper its spirit.

*

Rights are reserved,
liability disclaimed.
Prisoners' last words

are contrite
and pre-recorded.
Their code of justice

roughly translates: a tooth
for a camel-hair coat,
an eye for a Toyota.

*

Fish: the food of the devil.
Also, those afflicted
by an unaccountable sadness,

an *ennui*
without rhyme or reason,
a joyless desolation

bordering
on the psychopathic, are said
to be dreaming of fish.

*

Knowing as we do
their temperate habits,
their love of children and animals,

their outstanding contributions
in the field of traditional
music and dance, how can we

give credence
to their alleged involvement
in the events at Wadi Haar?

*

At dusk among the baobab trees
or in broad day,
enchanting you

with their broken English,
les petits voleurs
slipping their fingers

under, between, inside –
who steal your heart,
who clean you out.

*

By night, suddenly,
the Blowman will come.
Directly above the spot

where he will ejaculate
the glorious seed of the ancestors
into the sand,

a cloud in the shape
of *Phoenix dactylifera*
will mushroom in the sky.

*

Sundown. Cooking smells,
diesel oil. The dunes
a darkening mauve.

A low-flying Mirage
rips the sky in two
along a dotted line –

in one half djinns, fabulous creatures,
in the other the eye
of a desert storm.

*

The cache
of lighter fuel, soda siphons
and stolen cheque books

found in a ditch
by H. du Plessix Smith
is not, as previously supposed,

a bluff, a feint
to put off tomb-robbers,
but the real thing.

IN THE MIDDLE ATLAS

I wore the same clothes for eight days running,
some nights slept in them, some nights didn't sleep at all.
Like a Greek chorus, the dogs in the villages barked
but kept their distance, a stone's throw.

I talked to fewer and fewer people, but more intense:
a man who was Jesus, a woman who growled.
My own voice
was barely audible, I had to repeat everything twice.

The first hour in the city was like a gatecrashed party –
then a party upstairs or across the street...
One morning I counted the girls
I would have paid all the money I had to sleep with,
and in the afternoon the ones I wouldn't.

I climbed the hundred and ninety-nine steps
of the ruined minaret without pausing for breath.
Cars made way, women took their children in hand
so I could land without causing undue damage.

DRY GOODS

The dumb Swede is buying canvas.
Mrs Fitzpatrick can't decide between the blue and the pink.
Looking sheepish and old and naked
the sheriff wants a new pin for his badge.

A train, abandoned by its mother, utters a mournful wail.
The Carson brothers have shot nobody dead for a week.
The frontier between good and evil
is defended with linen, bonnets and balls of twine.

Nothing disturbs the noonday quiet
except the snores of Judge O'Halloran
and a scratching under the stairs,
the errand boy playing with matches.

FIGURINE

I like too
the shape you make
when you're trying on a new little something,
when facing away
from the full-length mirror
you hollow your back,
make a half-turn
so that the heel of one foot's lifted up,
and look appraisingly down
to observe the effect
from behind –
as if you're following yourself
home
incognito.

STRONGBOW

> I saw no wild or independent Indian... but now and again at
> way-stations, a husband and wife and a few children, disgracefully
> dressed out with the sweepings of civilisation, came forth and
> stared upon the emigrants.
> – R. L. Stevenson, *The Amateur Emigrant*

Two hours by Intercity north of London
I recall for no good reason
the cider-wrecked hobo

who waved me off, or away... And another
of his tribe, a whiskery ex-army tramp
who one dark and stormy night

drank my place dry, tried to clamber
into my bed, then broke down weeping
over a grimy letter –

its business logo, a closed portcullis –
from Enoch Powell, to whom he'd written applauding
the speech about rivers of blood.

Flatlands: thorny fields, ditches being dredged,
a woman out walking her dog...
The cooling towers. The burial grounds.

WHITE CITY

They will be selling our clothes, I know that now.
Our biscuit tins. Our boxing gloves.
Our rolls of surplus wallpaper.
Our tools and gardening equipment, hammers
and rusted sickles and the rake with bent tines.
Our model soldiers.
Our wireless set, on which we listened
to the national anthem and the racing results from Catterick.
Our loved ones and anniversaries
and twilit landscapes in their rickety frames; our books,
bookshelves, light-bulbs even, our watches
that stopped on our wrists.

They will have laid them all out
in rows or piles on groundsheets or trestle tables
or in the backs of hatchback cars.
It will be early in the morning
on the day of our Lord, the sky too will look blotched,
stained, used and abused, a wind out of it
rapidly losing patience. And not
that we'll need them or care a damn who owns them,
but small chemical reactions
we might another day ignore will make it imperative
we buy them back, haggling a little
until the price is right.

SHEDS

The way weeds and stiff grasses have reclaimed the yard,
the way the tracks lead frankly nowhere;
the dry rust, the continuous mockery
of insects, of birds; the way the toolsheds
could still be nothing but toolsheds
even without their tools, with their corners smelling of shame
and their little piles of filth...

Exhaustion, waste, relief
at being one again with nature –
and still a kind of reckless belief
that just one more day, another hour of light
would have seen it through.

from *The Age of Cardboard and String* (2001)

A RESPECTABLE NEIGHBOURHOOD

I was walking with irregular strides, avoiding
the cracks in the pavement and keeping a weather eye open
for the humdrum but telling detail –
the one I could never make up,
the proof that I tell no lie –
when this woman starts screaming blue murder
from an upper window. *Fuck you!*
she was yelling, and meaning it, and only stopped
to draw breath when I came to a stop myself.

A black-haired beauty, souls
have been sold for less.
I was flattered but about to move on
when she threw down a blue checked shirt –
followed by, in random order, pants,
jeans, a jumper and scuffed leather jacket,
half a dozen compact discs
and a copy of *La Chartreuse de Parme*
that, when it hit the ground, fell open
at chapter twenty-one, 'A Strange Encounter'.

The window slammed shut.
The sun ducked behind a bank of clouds.
A man dressed too smartly for comfort
stepped out of the doorway and gave me a look
that implied I should make myself scarce.

Will Fabrizio escape from the citadel?
Will Clelia cheat on her vow
never to set eyes on him again?
As I bent to retrieve the book
I felt like a thief of dead men's boots
on the field at Waterloo.

HOTEL ROSA

In the open briefcase
of the man across the aisle
on the bus from the airport
lies the manuscript of my poems.

I keep sneaking glances,
wondering about that haircut.

As we cross the lagoon,
and a smell of decaying fish
pervades the bus,
he turns to face me
with the look of one interrupted
by yet another of the pointless
bureaucratic intrusions
to which travellers are prone.

*

The style, Herr Fischer remarks of A—,
over our breakfast omelette
under the jacaranda tree
at the Hotel Rosa,
is that of a man
whose work has been translated
into forty-two languages
and then back into English.

His fingers are long and bony
but heavy on the keys.
From his room overlooking the garden
bouts of regular typing
alternate with curious bleats.

*

Two lime-green Sunbeam taxis
idle outside the gate.
One driver is asleep,
the other reminds me
of a tennis ex-pro
my father once packed me off to
after school, to practise my backhand.

I can't write a thing…
Herr Fischer has asked me
for a list of my favourite songs.

*

Sleep deprivation
may account for my headache today.
Last night, as we sat on the verandah
counting the fireflies,
an almighty splashing –
then a tall red-bearded man
came stumbling towards us,
shaking water off his clothes
like a wet dog.

Lawrence has arrived
with his difficult wife.

*

The Lawrences, Herr Fischer and I
shared a taxi to the open-air museum.
'The working model
of the funicular railway
(the original having been damaged
beyond repair) was made
by the metalwork class
of the boys' reformatory...'

Somehow I lost the others
and then got lost myself.
I am writing this
in a bar near the harbour,
surrounded by naked women
and drunken Chinese sailors.
Rarely have I been so happy.

*

Herr Fischer's birthday.
A storm that came out of nowhere
has cut off the electricity.
We play cards by candlelight
with the hotel proprietor,
who lost an arm in the war.
(*Which* war? I keep meaning to ask.)

In the yard at the back for cars
Lawrence is attempting to light a fire
of unseasoned wood
to spit-roast a kid.
Rain at the window again...
I feel certain that Frieda is cheating.

*

Lawrence at a loss for words!
Going down to the lobby
to ask for a plug for the bath,
I find him failing to convince
an itinerant vendor
of the worth of his Seiko watch.

He seems none too sure himself
of the provenance
of the mahogany statuette he desires.

*

Is it something I said?
Herr Fischer is avoiding me.
All day I've been carrying around
the money I owe him
from our game of pontoon.

*

So quiet this morning.
Alone in the dining room,
I very gently banged the gong.
There followed a shriek of laughter
from behind the kitchen door.

Herr Fischer and Lawrence
have departed upriver
on the trail of dark gods,
leaving me to cope as I can
with poor Frieda.

FOLLAIN'S LEEDS

Dead men walk down Briggate,
men killed by heavy machinery,
in boating accidents,
by diseases of body or mind.

Men killed on the Somme,
their faces chewed by rats,
stroll down Briggate
with all the time in the world.

One enters a barber's shop
and takes his place before a mirror
in which, behind him, a boy can be glimpsed
sweeping the hairs on the floor.

SEVEN POEMS FROM PROSE BY STENDHAL

The War Office

> At the end of the garden were some unfortunate, heavily pruned
> lime-trees, behind which we used to go to pee. They were the first
> friends that I had in Paris.
> – Stendhal, *La Vie de Henry Brulard*

I watched my pee soak into the soil –
so quickly, so eagerly did the trees drink it up,
no one, it seemed, had loved them as I.

My fingers were black
from the writing of letters – to this or that
quartermaster, to absconding paymasters,
kindly requesting… I too,
I said to myself, will one day wax my moustache,
sprout epaulettes, take an Italian opera singer
for my mistress – we will send the hussars north,
the dragoons south, campaign medals
will be struck.

Piqued
by my lack of attention, my friends
would become agitated, shaking leaves and birds
from their stunted branches
and setting up a wind
that travelled, for all I know, as far as Grenoble.
Gradually, reluctantly even,
they grew quiet and still, wondering
at their own strength.

Crossing the Saint-Bernard

During our evening halts he began to pass on to me some of
the principles of swordsmanship. 'Otherwise you'll get yourself
skewered like a…' I've forgotten the term of comparison.
– Stendhal, *La Vie de Henry Brulard*

La gloire of the sunsets!
Our blades flashing
in the high mountain air!
Clouds drenched in the colour –
it comes back to me now –
of ice in the gutter
outside the slaughterhouse.

In the Town of X

When I arrive in a town I always ask: 1. Who are the twelve
prettiest women? 2. Who are the twelve richest men? 3. Which
man could have me hanged?
– Stendhal, *Souvenirs d'Egotisme*

The apprentice stylist, wiping the mirrors
in the empty salon,
then inspecting her gums;

the sisters in the orchard;
their seasoned mother; the outspoken
librarian, biting her lip through the day;

the homesick exchange student,
her reddened eyes and perfect shrug;
the miscast Lady Macbeth,
chain-smoking in the green room;

the cardinal's daughter;
the dental hygienist with flu;
the undertaker's widow;

and the woman in Zeno's patisserie
like the woman in that painting by Manet
behind the bar, bored
by the whiskers and paintbrushes of men –

little shivers of happiness
as one by one each places her hand
on the bevel of my hip,

while the chief of police
and eleven other rich men
jangling their keys, ordering more brandy,
avert their eyes.

*

Rainy afternoons,
we trail through the furniture emporium:
so much chrome, veneer and lacquer
gives us a headache, we want to lie down…

Or we take in a matinee at the temperance hall
by The Man Who Has All The Answers:
patient and exact, he fields every question
as if no one has asked it before.

The sky afterwards is overwhelmingly bright –
like matrimony, like just having bought something
you've saved up for for years,
or a stage-set for an execution.

Sunday

Ah, it's Sunday, I say to myself. Instantly any inner tendency
towards happiness vanishes.
– Stendhal, *La Vie de Henry Brulard*

Leeds win away, and a man outside the newsagent's
mumbling *Merry Christmas! Merry Christmas!*

though it's already early March,
and they've left it too late for a place in Europe.

I hunker back to bed
to lick my belovèd's nipples

while she reads aloud from 'The Work of Art
in the Age of Mechanical Reproduction'.

The Picnic

> He was a very handsome young man, and spent his whole life in
> the woods with a hammer in his hand.
> – Stendhal, *La Chartreuse de Parme*

I lay down in the grass, replete.
Naked women flitted in and out of the trees.

Next time I looked, bandits with antique rifles
were creeping towards me.

*

Though my heart was beating
like the *tap-tap-tap*
of a tiny hammer, I remained quite calm.

They had not been bandits long
and had wives and children to support
and were lousy shots –

even when a rabbit
took pity, and made itself
a sitting target, they missed.

*

Pedro was wounded. I tied the picnic rug
to two branches, and dragged him into the shade.

He told me about his childhood sweetheart
to whom he sent letters in code
that were intercepted.

About the bullets fired into the air
at weddings, and about the naked women.

*

Never to be alone again
among the apple cores and beakers
with a wind getting up, raising the paper napkins
like flags of surrender...

*

I wrote down his last wish
and buried it under a stone.

Rainy Days

We were in the country, it was pouring with rain, and we were only too happy to listen to her.
— Stendhal, *De l'amour*

Dogs stop padding about, children
fretting, even the servants
replacing buckets
under the leaking gallery roof
become rapt, becalmed.

Soup is brought in,
lobster bisque. Blankets,
logs. I make furtive exits
to shake off my pins and needles,
to see to the horses,
to check the closing prices...

By the third day
the water is up to our ankles.
On the sixth, the abbé's bloated,
drifting corpse
becomes snagged on the piano stool.

Is she making this up, I wonder,
as she goes along?
Sometimes I turn the volume right down,
watch her mouth sweet nothings –

like rain on the sea,
or the continuous wavering *shhhhh*
of traffic on the motorway
across two fields.

The Disguise

> During the crossing it occurred to me that by wearing green
> spectacles and changing my coat I could quite well spend two or
> three days at Volterra, going out only at night and without being
> recognised by you.
> – Stendhal, letter to Matilde Dembowski, 11 June 1819

So that you wouldn't know I was following you,
I wore a second-hand coat and green sunglasses.
I arrived on the 3rd. It was open day
at the asylum, madmen were out on the streets
canvassing for the ruling party. A plush hotel
rented rooms by the hour; in the lobby, secret policemen
posed as gypsies selling lucky charms.
Priests were suspicious, bank managers friendly:
I seemed young and single and on the make.
I entered a café where others of my kind
were gathered in disguise: an eye patch or glass eye,
a toupée or false moustache. Women too,
smoking cigars. (So that no one might know I loved you,
I never spoke your name. So that no one might know
you did not love me back, I became a wit, a raconteur,
a boulevardier.) We debated pre-Columbian art,
heatedly. The pots in the archaeological institute
are fakes, every one of them, even the shards.
The real ones are kept in the livery stables,
packed in dry manure. The town was a hothouse,
though the sky was grey. I was so lathered in sweat
I couldn't sleep. I gave my coat to a beggar
outside the Selci Gate, a veteran of the Somme.
I took off my glasses. I had everything to lose.

RUSSIANS

They live, in general, on the fourth floor (the fourth floor of the
translator, which is usually the third floor for us Italians, or French
or Germans). They walk not up and down but from one corner to
another.
    – Aldo Buzzi, *Journey to the Land of the Flies*

I was briefly a guest of the Russians
before I became a machinist, and had to move out.
I still miss my handmade boots (pity the Catholics,
living below!), and not having to shave.

From the seventh floor you can see as far as the ring road,
but we machinists had little time to enjoy the view.
Anything except work was illegal,
as the work was too.

For now I have found my level among the *petite bourgeoisie*
who live above their shops and workshops
on the first (or, as the Americans have it, the second) floor.

We repair upholstery and sell magazines
that propagate our strange but true beliefs:
that egg yolk is good for the scalp,
that love conquers all.

On summer nights
the strains of drinking songs
drift down from above.
On winter mornings I sometimes think

that if I was not already married
I would like to marry the Cossack girl with pigtails
out foraging for fuel
for their wood-burning stoves.

THE AGE OF CARDBOARD AND STRING

It is a machine for eating oranges.
It is a machine for humming new tunes.
It is a rocket bound for the moon.
It is, whichever string you pull, the same machine.

When it breaks we apply more sellotape,
and when it breaks again we sulk, mixing our tears
into the glue. When it works

we set off for the moon,
scattering orange peel on the floor
and singing songs not yet written down –
hot, fierce songs

that almost burn our mouths with their newness.

*

Faster! Faster! We want to overtake
Anna, who is seven. We want

gears, automatic transmission, wings, clouds
to fly through, flags, fuel injection,
solar panels, stabilisers, sometimes just
to be left alone.

And no,
it wasn't us (with crumbs on our lips)
who stole the cookies from the cookie jar.

Maybe God.
Maybe God was hungry.

*

The moon was OK.
There were holes in it,
we saw biscuits and things at the bottom.

It was raining, the cardboard melted.
Tomorrow can we build a boat?

Wait! We brought you back a secret,
but we're going to tell it to the zebras first –
the black one with stripes painted white,
the white one with stripes painted black,

who sleep on the landing,
leaving just enough room to squeeze by.

THEORIES OF THE LEISURE CLASS

The office of the leisure class in social evolution is to retard the movement, and to conserve what is obsolescent.
— Thorstein Veblen, *The Theory of the Leisure Class* (1899)

That standing to attention for the national anthem never did us any harm.
That nor did boiled cabbage and burnt toast, despite its being carcinogenic.
That food wrapped in clingfilm lowers your sperm count.

That men under average height are more aggressive.
That it's something in the brake fluid that causes it.
That science can explain everything.

That what goes up must trickle down.
That we have come a long way since semiology.
That where would we be now but for the nuclear deterrent and the fear of God.

That we all know what married men are like.
That divorce counsellors with beards come from broken homes.
That sleeping with the light on makes you go blind.

That getting and spending is good for the thighs and lower back.
That profits from the sale under licence of the gene for happiness will transform the marketplace.
That the welfare state is all very well.

That in the future, we will live for ever.
That irony is a finite resource.
That looters should be shot on sight.

14TH FEBRUARY STREET

Valentine's Day, and my lips are sealed.
But I will say this: that the balloons
tethered to the railing outside a basement wine bar
advertising Happy Hour 5 to 7,
two drinks for the price of one –
that these heart-shaped helium-filled fluorescent balloons
which rise and sag, shiver and crinkle
according to the draughts of passing traffic,
according to the weather in the street,
remind me of those other ads for lump-sum investments
with small print at the bottom you're hardly meant
to read: can go down as well as up.

LONG STORY SHORT

1 *Early Days*

Pilots crash-landed. Arms were devoured
by threshing-machines. Grown men bitten by snakes
died in agony
within twenty-four hours, while children
simply vanished – she was down
by the river washing clothes, she was heating up beans
in the kitchen, she screwed up her eyes
and cupped a hand above her brows and stared
past the cemetery, past the telegraph station,
but she knew they were gone.

On the other hand, God existed.

On the other hand, she sat in the shade for years
whittling sticks
into curious knotted shapes
with mouths and ears, penises and vaginas
and other organs
I no longer recall.

2 *The Boom Years*

When he wanted to sober up
he drove to the top of Beacon Hill
with a couple of beers and his woman
and watched the money rolling in.

The lights. The glitz. The *boom-boom*
of the nightclub bass and the round-the-clock mills
and the ache in his jaw
after her husband caught them in bed.

The taste, salty and sweet,
of the patch behind her earlobe
he kept coming back to for more.

3   *The Flipper People*

Encumbered as we are –
with buckets and spades, swimwear, towels,
picnic boxes, bronzing lotions, paperback biographies
and glossy magazines in which minor royalty
reveal the secrets of their wardrobes –
we wear the flippers, it seems easier than carrying them.

Flip-flop we go across a muddy field
in perfect iambs
to the shingle beach. Flip-flop.

The sun will bake the mud hard.
Later, light falls of volcanic ash will cover
and preserve our flipper prints, so that you among others
will draw the wrong conclusions.

CASUAL WORK

When our children try to read between the lines
of our autograph books, we tell them about the year
the angels held their convention
at the Station Hotel.

Their debates on revisionist heresies
and minimum wingspans
passed over our heads, and we failed to seduce even one,
but we carried their Samsonite briefcases.

We fixed up the overhead projector.
We replenished their bottled water.
We recommended seafood restaurants.
We aired their rooms.

MOONLIGHTING

It's later than you think. The waiter yawns.
The cook, the under-cook, the barman, the trainee
manager who's barely out of school, all yawn.
Then the woman in the tricky blue blouse –
shamelessly, with all her heart – and the delegates
from the menswear conference who are on expenses,
with the drinks bill to prove it, the bald man
reading Dickens and the German mum-and-dad-
and-two-bored-teenagers, also the pasty man
sitting opposite the woman in blue, checking his watch.
His wife too – you'd think this yawn
would have tired itself out, would be raising one hand
to its opening mouth, but no – his wife at home
in the bedroom doorway, her weight against the jamb,
watching their only child asleep. The doorman
downstairs, the conductor on the night bus
passing by, even the Pope, on the TV behind the bar,
is yawning, 2,000 years of Christianity and still
they don't get it, Europe, the Western world
baring its wet pink gums
and livid tongue, as if slowly beginning
to turn itself inside out...
        While I, in a borrowed apron
behind the swing-doors, scrape half a raspberry pavlova
into the bin and plunge the plate
into scummy water (a white-collar man by day,
I am seized at times by an urgent need
to do something manual, something involving dirt).

MY OVERTHROW

Bandits from the hills infiltrated the town.
They sold blood-red roses at busy intersections,
whispering through the windows of rush-hour traffic
sublime promises, subversive rumours. They loitered
in stairwells, telling jokes with slow-burning punchlines.
They trained stray dogs to follow me to work
and stand by my office door, whimpering softly.
They handed out fliers for public executions.
They hummed continuous loops of martial music.
They forged my signature and ordered in my name
high-quality luxury goods: an electric wheelchair,
a commemorative dinner service, a shredding machine
into which I fed the instruction manual and three-year
guarantee and – in error, in my eagerness to please –
my life-savings certificates. They played football
on the palace lawn and deliberately kicked the ball
into the path of my car, forcing me to swerve violently
and run over a cat – its eyes softened
in recognition, its entrails were spotted with black.

I got home late. On the mantelpiece,
a single rose, every petal intact. I took off my clothes
and folded them neatly, how I'd folded them for years:
lean years and fat, fallow, madcap, *démodé* years
of unclassifiable material, half eaten by moths,
swaying when I breathed, with the indelible smell of me.

AN ABERRATION

Something about, something to do with…
Hard to recall just now

quite what we were speaking of
before that couple of show-off police cars

and a stark raving ambulance
came blaring by, drowning us out,

carving a bully-boy path
through the meek mid-morning traffic –

and not entirely blameless too
the man with the cardiac arrest

or the child who climbed over a fence
and got a high electric dose

or the woman whose contractions came on
so suddenly, *ambushed* her really,

catching her unawares – something
about, something to do with the shape

of your neck…

SKADARLIJA

This was the café I'd go to
when I couldn't stand being in the same house as the person
or persons I'd just quarrelled with
and the temperature was below freezing
and I'd left my lighter in the pocket of my other jacket.
Fortunately there were heavy smokers there
from whom I could bum a light
and then another, as I sat at the counter by the window
nursing my hot cup of self-righteousness
and looking out at the snow drifting down but not settling,
as it rarely does in cities, sudden flurries or eddies
and the people so intent and wrapped up
they might have been sleepwalking. I could sit here
happily, I remember thinking – while the men around me
who greeted one another like brothers, as if they'd all grown up
in one household, one rambling overpopulated villa
down an unpaved lane, students and refugees and local
entrepreneurs, chess-playing grandfathers and always at least
one beautiful woman, talked in their language
and ignored me – I could sit here happily
for the rest of my life; but it may be I was only waiting
for the flower-seller to come in through the door
with his bunches of ready-wrapped roses, tulips even,
which to last a little longer
should be cut diagonally and crushed across the stem
before they are placed in water.

CABIN FEVER

Abandoning the aircraft: open cockpit door. Disconnect
intercommunication lead and undo safety harness. Slide over the
side, head foremost and facing the tail.
– *Pilot's Notes for Tiger Moth Aircraft* (RAAF, 1944)

A buzz in the air, in her head, disturbing
what was hardly a train of thought.
Something to be fixed, attended to...

He comes in low, skimming the trees
from which shrill black birds rise up in alarm
as the engine coughs, stutters, then gives up the ghost.

*

It's to do with age, she thinks, with obsolescence.
She's standing in this little hut
by the runway, not touching anything –
oil-drums, tools, trays of bolts and wing-nuts,
old grease-stained maps and manuals,
two unwashed mugs, a stack of magazines
dating, she just knows, from the early Fifties:
a place a man might now and then
step into, take what he wants
and leave, forgetting to lock the door.

*

At the governor's reception
he stands stock still, rooted
to the parquet floor, balancing his glass of cloudy wine
and his plate of tidbits, on the one hand innocence,

on the other experience, while the breasts
of jasmine-scented women brush lightly by him
and the governor's ten-year-old daughter
runs in circles with arms outstretched,
making aeroplane noises.

*

Once, he tells her, setting the oil-can
back on the shelf, wiping the grease off his hands,
he flew to America. He was driven by limousine
into Manhattan. He had just sat down
in the fourth-floor lounge
of his budget hotel, a bourbon in his hand,
when a suicide fell past the window.

Or the time the ailerons jammed with ice
at 11,000 feet, and when he hit a spot of turbulence
the whole thing skewed, bucked
and went into a corkscrew dive, spinning,
unravelling, until, falling through
beneath the clouds, no more than 50 feet above the waves,
he opened the throttle and levelled out.

*

The people of the Celebes opened their hearts:
the runway was garnished with pale blue flowers.
The people of Chiang Mai were nervous
and those of Dakar, generous to a fault.
Of Denver, depressed. Of Kandahar

and also Wuzhou, ambidextrous. In Vientiane
the streets were deserted, it was a holiday
for the dead, even the dead
need a change of air, a time to unwind.

*

This morning the sky is overcast
and they're doing some routine maintenance:
tightening the rigging,
adjusting the rudder pedals.

She walks towards him, scratching her left upper arm.
He is wiping his hands on a rag.

Afterwards, after the ground crew have dispersed
and enough time has elapsed
for her to remove her glasses
and change into a light summer frock
that leaves her shoulders bare,
he plans to tell her the truth.

*

She's been closing her eyes, she's been landing
in a mellow dune
close by a watering hole
where zebras congregate at dusk –

she can hear them drinking, sucking rather,
until the daylight has utterly gone
and the white of their stripes –

she's been telling herself
life doesn't happen like this
except sometimes, which is why
the emergency services seem under-rehearsed.

THE WELLINGTON GROUP

The term refers to a loose association of New Zealand poets in Wellington, in the years between 1950 and 1965... Certainly James K. Baxter and Louis Johnson, both Wellington residents during the period, seemed to draw a number of poets around them: Alastair Campbell, for example, and the immigrants Peter Bland and Charles Boyle.
– *The Oxford Companion to Twentieth-Century Poetry* (1994)

Remind me, Peter,

what was on the agenda – weren't we trying to prove a point
to the eggheads up in Auckland

about truth to experience, the sacredness
of where and when and who?

Since I returned to London in nineteen-whatever
to start all over, to write my *bildungsroman*

of a wild colonial boy
in the new Elizabethan age, I seem to have lost touch

almost with my own life: my children look at me
as if across a genetic barrier,

and did I really sleep with Miss South Island
'63, or was that something else

I made up for the c.v.? But sometimes, Peter,
after lunch with my agent

in a restaurant where not even the cloakroom attendant
pretends he knows me, I'm there again –

among the bottles and books and rhyming voices
in a draughty upstairs room

where James K. Baxter holds me on his knee.
I am four years old. I don't want to go to bed.

THE BODY DOUBLE

Also that look
you give me, as if I was someone famous
you'd chanced upon in Tesco,

but somehow less tall, young, sexy or dead
than you'd supposed, maybe even
not me after all, not the one, say,

in *The English Patient*
who carries Kristin Scott Thomas
out of the cave, but the one in the ad

for Renault cars, or was it Ford.

THE PRIVILEGES
(after Stendhal)

Arriving in small towns where both hotels are full,
may I find that a room in the prettier one
has unexpectedly become available.
May this room have a balcony, a bed with a firm mattress,
a selection of my favourite books from thirty years ago
and a telephone that will bring me the voice
of a former lover, now resident in this town
 with a rich, complaisant husband and a fondness
for shellfish, basil, garlic and Parmesan.

*

At home or abroad, may I be able to converse
fluently and with the correct accent in the language
of whomever I am addressing. Such fluency
in foreign tongues to be extended to the writing of letters,
but not to any work intended for publication.

*

May I be permitted to park on double yellow lines
without penalty, to pay no income tax
and to write one decent poem every six weeks.
May my bowel movements, waterworks and sexual
competence remain untrammelled by age or disease.

*

Every so often may I get off my arse
and join in the game in the park and surprise myself
by performing some feat of unparalleled natural-born skill
which the others will take for granted.
May children entrust to me
astounding secrets which I will never betray.

*

Three times a year may I sleep past my stop on the tube
and become, for as long as it amuses me, a woman.
Midwinter weekday mornings, a love letter would be nice:
a real one, something I have to live up to. And besides
all that – remembering six good jokes and never losing my keys
or having to queue – may I be continually surprised
by whatever happens next.

SUMMER, AN AFTERNOON

Summer, an afternoon, with time to kill,
I enter the bar behind the abbey
and there by the window is my love
at a table for two, writing postcards.

She has been busy (I am reading
over her shoulder, I am nibbling
her salted almonds, I am licking her stamps
with the portrait of Henry the Navigator).

She has bought a leather coat
and cannot imagine when she will wear it.
She has been to the art gallery
three times, and in that rushed, familiar hand
she wonders why it is
she is so drawn to paintings that are dark, and late,
and to which the photos on the reverse fail to do justice.

I reach across to offer her a light.
She misses everyone…
I reach across to offer her a light

or share her wine or touch
her cheek or add my bit along the bottom edge
or in the margin, but this poem
is closing now, the waiters
are checking their watches, the abbey
is being rolled up, oxygen levels are critical
as we leave hurriedly through a small back room
containing crates of empty bottles,
knives, a mirror, a cat curled like an ammonite
on a three-legged chair.

AUTHOR'S NOTE

A *Selected Poems* arriving twenty years after I stopped writing poems, and the choice of which poems are in here and which not made by someone other than myself – I can't help but feel there's something posthumous about this. A message from the Other Side: I am deeply grateful to Christopher Reid, who has made this selection and who ushered me into Faber for the last two books; to Michael Schmidt, who published the earlier work with Carcanet; and to Natalia Zagórska-Thomas for the cover.

Why did the poems stop? A blazing row with the Muse? It was actually more of an amicable separation. In theory, the longer you practise a certain form of writing, the more capable you become of bringing into the writing material that would resist a more inexperienced writer, but in my case that wasn't happening. I was writing poems I had *already written*, so I got off the bike. I started writing prose, and found I could do things with that I couldn't do in poetry. Many other poets have found this to be so (Grace Paley and Kenneth Koch among them); most of them carry on writing both poetry and prose, but I can only do one thing at a time.